To Wuenn
Dean

May this book
bless you

Courtney
Brook

9/19/15

S.H.E.

SERENITY, HOPE, & ENCOURAGEMENT

For Daily Motivation

COURTNEY BROOKS

WESTBOW°
PRESS
A DIVISION OF THOMAS NELSON
& ZONDERVAN

Scripture taken from the King James Version of the Bible.

Scripture quotations are from The Holy Bible, English Standard Version® (ESV®), copyright © 2001 by Crossway, a publishing ministry of Good News Publishers. Used by permission. All rights reserved.

WestBow Press books may be ordered through booksellers or by contacting:

WestBow Press
A Division of Thomas Nelson & Zondervan
1663 Liberty Drive
Bloomington, IN 47403
www.westbowpress.com
1 (866) 928-1240

ISBN: 978-1-4908-7833-1 (sc)
ISBN: 978-1-4908-7832-4 (hc)
ISBN: 978-1-4908-7834-8 (e)

Library of Congress Control Number: 2015906990

Print information available on the last page.

WestBow Press rev. date: 05/05/2015

This book is dedicated to anyone whose dreams
are drowned out by the voices of doubt.

For anyone who is striving to be better than
the person they were yesterday.

For those who have dreams that they want to accomplish,
but are disappointed by those who don't believe in you.

For those who need daily motivation when they sometimes
can't seem to find the strength within to continue the journey.

This book is for those believers who never stopped
believing even when hope seemed so distant.

This is for you.

Acknowledgements

First and foremost I give honor to God for instilling the gift of writing inside of me. Thank you for allowing me to look past my fear, and answer to my calling. I could not do it without you, and for that I am forever grateful!

My mother, Amy Wallace, for raising me to be an independent woman, and for always pushing me to reach for the stars. Thank you for always being there. I love you!

My siblings: Michael Taylor, I have watched you grow and outgrow me. Your moment is coming just trust God to lead your path.

Tierra Taylor, my princess, Jaylen & Justin Taylor, my two younger prince, one day you will be able to understand this book, and when you do I'll be here with any questions that you will have.

Jasmine Brooks and Jourdan Brooks read this book whenever you need encouragement, or if you just want to talk I'm always here. I love you all!!!

My sister Davina Hunt, I can't believe I've finally wrote the book!!! I've talked about it for so long, and now it's finally here. Thank you for listening to all the crazy ideas I came up with. You are the true definition of a real friend, and no one will ever take your place.

My brother Rozelle Green, Remember how I used to help you with your papers in college? Well, you owe me one. You too have always been a great friend, and a very honest and loyal person. Keep aiming for more, don't ever give up on anything your heart desires.

My editor, Tiffany Earvin for always being such an amazing inspiration in my life. Thank you for always pushing me towards my best because of your help I discovered the powers of using my fullest potential. There is no amount of gratitude that will express how grateful I am for that.

All of my family, friends, all of my cousins, aunts, uncles, grandma and grandpa on both sides of the family, I hope you all enjoy my first book. I would name you all, but it's too many!

Contents

Before You Begin....

Before you begin your journey into this book, let me ask you something: have you had your S.H.E. today? That is, your Serenity, Hope, and Encouragement. If not you have come to the right place! This book, contains thirty daily motivational messages to help instill courage into whatever area of your life you feel needs it most. You will see words like "faith", "defeat", "contentment", and "survivor". Bible verses complement the word of the day which provides a deeper insight on what that word actually means.

We, yes, you and I intensely dig into your emotions, goals, and dreams through exercises after each daily reading. Don't worry; they're not quizzes. The questions are there to help you obtain a better understanding of how to accomplish what your heart desires.

There will be days when you feel like giving up, when life lets you down. There will be days when you wonder if God is still listening to you, Trust me, he is. When those feelings emerge, pick up this book as a reminder that you have to remain motivated under all circumstances, no matter what problems you face. Remind yourself it is only a temporary situation. It will NOT last forever.

My goal is for you to feel inspired after each reading, motivated to accomplish whatever is on your list of goals, and for you to feel so empowered that you have confidence to handle any obstacle that may come your way. What are you waiting for? Go ahead and get your S.H.E on! Day 1 is waiting.....

Day 1

Let him turn away from evil, and do good;
Let him seek peace and pursue it

1 Peter 3:11

Serenity

God grant me the Serenity to accept the things I cannot change, Courage to change the things that I can, and Wisdom to know the difference. Amen.

Serenity is that sunshine on a cloudy day. It is that peaceful quietness when the world around you seems to be filled with noise. It is the gravity that keeps you grounded when you feel you are about to fly off due to stress or too many things pulling at you, demanding your attention. Serenity is the guard that soothes your soul and keeps your mind at ease.

We may feel troubled and imprisoned by our thoughts about life. As a child, you heard about the dangers of the world, but you never imagined it being as tedious as it is now. Over time you learn to adjust to things happening and not to make an issue out of everything. You learn that not every negative comment made by someone is worth your attention. You also learn that because someone's attitude towards you is negative doesn't mean you have to display a negative attitude towards that individual.

Serenity is something you grow into. In order, to do so, you must first discover the reason you need serenity. Is there something in your life that you need to change? Is there a certain individual, such as a person in your life who seems to drain your positive energy that you will need to be serene around?

You will need serenity to accept the changes in your life, when you can't gather the strength to accept them on your own. Serenity begins in your mind. If you can't alter your way of thinking, it will be difficult to change your behavior. Your thoughts control what you say and do.

When you grow into serenity, everything about you becomes different. You will be at peace with decisions you have made in life. You will be able to unhesistantly place your trust and issues in God's hands, because you know yours are way too small to hold all your problems together. Having serenity frees you from anything holding you back. When you grow into serenity, you become the peace-holder of your thoughts. You must be willing to accept peace into your life before you can truly enjoy it. Serenity is your sunshine on a cloudy day, and your forecast can be bright everyday if you change your perspective and allow yourself to see the sun.

What is your mood forecast for today?

Are you allowing yourself to feel serenity?

Day 2

And now, Oh Lord, for what do I wait? My hope is in you.

Psalm 39:7

Hope

Hope gives you the courage to believe all things are possible. You hope things will work in your favor. You may hope you win the lottery. You may even hope an ill family member gets better. It is hope that pushes you when you have more questions than answers, and feel like giving up.

Hope should not be perceived as a wish, but as confidence in expectation. It is the belief that everything will get better, even when you don't see any indication of improvement.

Nothing will seem impossible when you believe in hope. When you have hope you expect something great to happen, and you your faith to grow stronger.

Life's frustrations may make you feel like giving up, but believe in yourself and be mindful there is more joy in tomorrow. In a game of basketball, one missed free throw in the first quarter does not mean the team will have a bad game. In other words, one bad day or one bad situation does not determine how the rest of your life will play out.

You can't allow your emotions to defeat your hope. You can't allow fear to outweigh your faith. You can't allow yourself to feel like God is not working. He is always behind the scenes, putting the pieces of your life together in the order they belong.

If a well-trusted friend recommends a restaurant to you, you trust their judgment because you trust them. You may walk into that restaurant, scan the menu, and order your food. If the server does not write down your order, it's an indication to you that he or she has been there for a while, so you hope your order is correct.

You also hope the food is as good as your friend said it is. Deep down inside under all of that hope is knowing.

You know the server will remember because he or she has been doing it for a while. You know the food will be good because it was recommended by a friend. Just like you should know God will get it right because he's been doing it for a while, and you know he will do it right because you have witness him bless a friend.

Believe in your hope, and trust God. Everything will work itself out, even when you see no indication of it happening yet.

What do you hope for?

Why do you hope for it?

Day 3

For God gave us a spirit not of fear but of
power and love and self-control.

2 Timothy 1:7

Encouragement

Your days on Earth won't always be filled with sunshine and rainbows. Some days you won't feel like being bothered by people, or you may not feel like leaving your home at all.

When you feel a sense of gloom consuming you, and it doesn't make you feel like your normal, happy self, that's when you need to encourage yourself. At that moment, you need to remind yourself, "Today I am amazing, and I will conquer the day. I will not allow the day to conquer me."

You don't need validation from anyone to tell yourself you are wonderful. You should already feel wonderful. You don't need anyone to tell you that you can reach your fullest potential or that you can follow your dreams because you already know that. You don't need anyone to make you feel good about yourself because encouragement comes from within.

When you build confidence within yourself, you begin to understand your flaws and imperfections are part of who you are. If you learn to accept your flaws, it will be harder for people to tear you down.

You were beautifully and wonderfully created with the skin of diamonds, so if you do break, you are still valuable. Encouragement should be an essential part of your daily routine. I believe staying encouraged and helping others to stay encouraged can go a long way. You never know what storm someone is facing. That's why it is important to be kind to everyone.

It is helpful to develop self-control. By doing so, you will be able to control your thoughts, actions, and the encouragement that dwells in you. Learn to be your own encourager because when you need it the most, others may not be around to provide it for you.

You are unique. You are intelligent. You are creative. Start today by stating three characteristics you love about yourself, and watch the change brew inside you. Today, you will conquer the day; you will not allow the day to conquer you.

List three characteristics about yourself that you love.

What are you doing to encourage others?

Day 4

But he himself went a day's journey into the wilderness and came and sat down under a broom tree. And he asked that he might die, saying, "It is enough; now, O Lord, take away my life, for I am no better than my fathers."

1 Kings 19:4

Defeat

Whenever you try to accomplish anything in life, you are going to hear a thousand no's before hearing one yes. That one no can stir up so many thoughts of confusion and doubt within you. It can have such a powerful effect in your mind that you begin to think your dreams don't matter anymore. You may feel defeated.

Feelings of defeat can appear like a thief in the night. One day you may feel so motivated you believe you can conquer all your goals at one time. The next day thoughts of defeat can enter your mind, and make you forget why you were motivated in the beginning.

I didn't always feel like writing books or encouraging others, but I did it anyway. I didn't always receive the recognition I thought I deserved while engaging in the writing of statuses on social media. As a result, I felt defeated trying to gain the attention of followers. I would only receive few likes on my posts. If I would have placed my focus on being defeated, I wouldn't have been able to fulfill my dreams as a writer.

You can't allow the false ideas of defeat to discourage you. Every day you should feel encouraged to do your best, encouraged to be your best, and encouraged to work towards your best.

Whenever those thoughts of defeat creep into the back of your mind, you can push them right back out by saying, "No, not today! I will not be defeated today." It is absolutely fine to give yourself a pep talk sometimes especially when it is necessary to do so. If you can't encourage yourself, then don't expect anyone else to do it for you either.

You have to be your biggest cheerleader by cheering defeat out of your life, and cheer victory right into your life. You have to remain motivated, furthermore, you have to remain consistent if you want to become that person that you dream of being.

Don't allow defeat to make you take a detour from your goals, instead use it for motivation to stand against all negative energy that comes your way, and remember to say "No, not today! I will not be defeated today."

What makes you feel like you have been defeated?

How can you overcome those feelings?

Day 5

Trust in the Lord with all your heart, and do not lean unto your own understanding.

Proverbs 3:5

Journey

Can you imagine how dull your life would be if the one gift you had was the exact same gift as everyone else? What if we were all placed on Earth for the same mission? How would any of us accomplish anything? God has given us our own unique paths to follow in life. What is interesting is no one's journey is ever the same.

If everyone was placed on earth to become actors, who would produce the movie? Who would write the screen plays? Most importantly, who would sit in the audience? We are all unique individuals with personalized gifts given to us by our creator. Each of us are placed on individual life paths, so we can venture out into different directions. What's good for someone else's life may not necessarily be good for yours. Their journey comes along with completely different directions. You will lose sight of your journey once you begin to compare it with the journey of someone else.

There were times where I would view the lives of others, and I would wonder, "Lord why is this not happening to me? I am praying consistently, but when will my moment arrive?"

In my mind, I was ready to receive blessings, but God had better plans in store. He knew if he gave me the blessings before it was time for me to receive them, I wouldn't have been as prepared for them as I thought.

When you are driving on the street, you will approach traffic lights. When the light changes from yellow to red, you know you have to come to a complete stop, despite the speed you are driving. While you are waiting, you may drive forward just a little bit at a time, out of anxiousness. You cannot move until the light turns green again. Driving any time before the light changes colors, can result in an accident that could have been avoided if you were being patient. The timing has to be right before you can move forward. The same process applies for your blessings. The timing has to be right before you can receive them, any time before that can cause issues that could have been avoided. You have to wait on God's green light before you can receive your blessings.

Your belief and trust in him will be an important part of the traveling process. You will need to pack faith, courage, wisdom, and patience with you wherever you go. Your journey is being navigated by God. You can never get lost when He is giving you directions.

It is important to remember that your journey is yours. You don't have to listen to anyone who is trying to rush you into finishing what you have started. As long as you allow God to lead your life, any path that you walk on will gleam with the gifts of your spirit.

Where would you like your journey to lead you?

Are you trusting God with leading your journey? If so, how are you allowing him to lead you?

Day 6

"I have said these things to you, that in me you may
have peace. In the world you will have tribulation,
but take heart; I have overcome the world."

John 16:33

Faith

To have faith simply means to trust God even when you are down to your last dime. You have to trust God past your fear. You have to believe that he will mend everything that has you on the edge of worry. When you make the decision to place your fears aside and your doubts on hold, you are allowing your faith to be activated. When you activate your faith, it does not mean your problems will disappear, but it means you are allowing God a chance to fix them for you.

When you are skeptical of how you're going to pay your bills, instead of worrying, utilize your faith by praying. When you don't know how you're going to make it from one pay check to the next, instead of worrying, praise Him anyway. That is how you use your faith.

Faith removes fear from your mind by adding courage to your heart. It is impossible for you to have faith and fear simultaneously. When trying to have both, it will be like mixing oil and water together. They just simply don't mix!

You should still have faith when you don't know where your blessing is coming from. I can recall a time about two years ago, before I purchased my first car, and before I rented my first apartment, where I would always tell my friends, "I'm going to get my car and my apartment this year." Surprisingly, I had no idea where I would get the finances to get a car or an apartment. I was confident in activating my faith, so I spoke the words into the atmosphere. Within that same year, I received my car and apartment, a month apart from one another. I did not allow the fear of financial woes to discourage me, and as a result my faith was activated, and I was blessed.

We tend to worry about issues that have already been resolved by God. You have to ask yourself, "If he has blessed me before, what makes me think that he would leave me stranded now?"

God is a loyal, faithful God, so when you pray, he hears you. He already knows the desires of your heart. You shouldn't focus your attention on what you do not have because he will supply you with what you need.

The smallest act of faith can release your blessings, and the smallest thought of fear can push back the release date. Stay positive and prayerful. He has already resolved your issues. Let go of fear, and activate your faith.

What are you trusting God to do for you?

List 3 ways that you are utilizing your faith.

Day 7

I know both how to have a little, and I know how
to have a lot. In any and all circumstances. I have
learned the secret of being content whether well fed
or hungry, whether in abundance or in need.

Philippians 4:12

Contentment

Throughout your life, you may run into obstacles that will make you overanalyze your faith in God. Those obstacles could also make you overanalyze your faith to get through them. The tests of your belief, will arrive to monitor how you would react if everything you have worked hard for was suddenly taken away from you. Would you still trust God to bless you with twice as much as you had before? Would you blame him for the sudden loss of items that can be easily replaced? Your happiness should not be based off of the material items that you possess.

Just ask yourself, if I lost my car or home would I still trust God? Would I still pray? Or would I thank him for what he is about to do for me now? God wants to know if you can stay encouraged even when you have become discouraged. He wants you to trust him even when you can't see why you are trusting him.

So what does it mean to truly be happy? What is the secret of everlasting happiness? The secret of contentment lies within your thoughts. The truth of the matter is, you really are what you think. If you think yourself into unhappiness, then you will become unhappy. If you think you are fantastic, then you will feel fantastic.

You don't want to think yourself into a bad mood because an idle mind is the devil's playground. He will swing those negative thoughts back and forward in your head until you're spinning around like a merry go round if you allow him.

It is an amazing feeling when you begin to relax your worries, and allow yourself to feel joy when you don't have much. If you're overwhelmed with joy when you don't have much, imagine what you'll do when you have much more!

A person who is homeless, may be deprived of food, and will go days without eating anything. A small order of French fries given to that individual by someone else could brighten their day. If the feeling of joy can come from receiving French fries, imagine the joy they would feel with a full combo meal in front of them. The smallest acts of kindness can bring a smile to any face.

You must remember to remain content with what you have, and learn to embrace the joy around you. Most of the time unhappiness may result from not being able to fulfill the desires of the heart. You may want something, but that does not mean you need it. Yes, God can answer no or not right now to some prayers because he always knows what's best. Don't allow your thoughts to create unwanted emptiness that wasn't there before by wishing for what you *think* you need.

Today take the time to look around at your family, friends, and your accomplishments. Take a look at your happiness and understand that it doesn't take much to enjoy that feeling.

When your faith is being tested, how do you
let God know that you trust him?

What are some things that make you content?

Day 8

If you want to know what God wants you to do ask him, and he will gladly tell you.

James 1:5

Present

In order for you to live an extraordinary life, you have to learn how to become an extraordinary person. Every step that you take in life will guide you towards the stair case of your future. Those who came before you did not get there in one step. What's amazing about those individuals is no matter how many flights of stairs they had to climb, they never stopped climbing until they reached the top.

Oprah wasn't born a billionaire. Barack Obama wasn't born the president, and an entrepreneur did not become a success over night. These individuals worked hard in the present moment because they knew they wanted to have a bright future.

Nothing worth having in life will come easy. Anything that comes easily will have an expiration date, which will not leave you with much time to enjoy it. Usually when something comes easy, it's a set up. Imagine if a check came in the mail with your name on it that said "Congratulations!! [Insert name] You have won $150,000!! All we need for you to do is to fill out your information on the document that has been provided, and return it within 2-5 business days to redeem your prize.

Do you see how suspicious that sounds? If it was that easy, we would all be rich. That's why it is important for you to work hard for what you want now regardless of what it is that you desire out of life. Do you want that promotion? You have to work hard now, so that you can get it later. Do you want your body to remain in good health when you get older? Then you have to take care of yourself now, so that you can be healthy later. Do you want to take that dream vacation that you always wished to take? Then you have to save now, so that you can enjoy it later.

The decisions you make in the present will give you great results in the future. All you have to do is believe in yourself, place your faith in God, and all things will come together.

If it comes too easy, then think of it as a trap. Don't place yourself in a position to walk into a set up. Set your life alarm clock to *forward*. Your main focus should be walking towards your future with nothing but your goals in mind.

God has given you a purpose for a reason. You have a purpose to live in the present. You have a purpose to walk into your destiny. You have a purpose to start becoming an extraordinary person now so that you can live an extraordinary life later. The future will be your greatest surprise, but the present will always be your most precious gift.

How are you using the present to prepare for the future?

How will the decisions that you make now, affect you later?

Day 9

Therefore if anyone is in Christ, there is a new creation,
old things have passed away, and new things have come.

2 Corinthians 6:17

Past

The past is dark for a reason, so that you can't use a light to find your way back there. When you make changes in your life, everything that you use to do have been washed away. You have a chance at starting over with a fresh, clean slate. You are not who you use to be, which is why you shouldn't let your past define who you are now.

You are much better than that person. You are stronger, wiser, and much more mature than that person. Your past will not eliminate you from receiving God's grace. When he wants to use you, he will still do so. If God used Moses who was a murderer, Peter who was quick tempered, Noah who was a drunk, and Elijah who was suicidal then certainly he can use you. Despite how dark your background might appear to be, God would still find use for you somewhere.

The mistakes you have made in the past, were only lessons that were preparing you to make wise decisions in the future. Now you should have the knowledge of understanding how the choices you make today will affect your tomorrow. The lessons you have learned is a part of the process in becoming a better you. Everyone has a past, so there is no need to be ashamed of yours.

When your mind begins to wonder off into that dark place, think about your past as an old wooden, dilapidated house. It's in the middle of a bad neighborhood with caution tape surrounding it. There is paint chipping off the walls. The grass in the front yard needs to be cut. The knob is missing from the front door. The windows are busted, and the shutters are hanging on for dear life! You wouldn't want to live there now would you?

Now think about your present, you're living in a new freshly painted home. The new home is in a nice neighborhood with a gate around it. The grass is freshly cut. The door knob is attached to the door, and doorbell is there as well. The windows are in great condition, and there are brand new shutters on them. That's how it feels when you accept Christ, and make changes into your life. You don't live in your past anymore. Instead, you move to a new neighborhood in a safer environment then where you used to be.

Sometimes it's the people surrounding you who will bring up your past. Do yourself a favor and press Alt + Del when those people come around. You don't need any reminders when you're trying to move forward with your life. Not everyone will be understanding of the new change. They don't have the vision God has given to you. They can't see where you are going, so it's hard for them to accept the new you. Remember you are here to please God, not man.

Your past is not who you are anymore, so don't let it cripple you in your future. All things are made new, and that includes you as well. You are not living in that dilapidated home anymore. You are living in a mansion now. If God can forget your sins, then why can't you? You are better than that image the past portrays you to be. You can make any changes in your life that you wish to, but you have to be willing to do so. Change begins with you.

*What pieces of your past are withholding you
from reaching your fullest potential?*

How has that/those experience(s) affected who you are now?

What methods are you utilizing to heal the left over hurt?

Day 10

Therefore don't worry about tomorrow, because tomorrow will worry about itself. Each day has enough trouble of its own.

Matthew 6:34

Focus

When you are driving down the street you have to focus on the road. You have to focus on the direction you are going. You have to focus on the lights as they change, and you have to remain focused to stay in your lane. The moment you lose that focus you could crash instantly. That's what could happen in life if you take your eyes off your goals. You may not crash, but you could miss the opportunity to make that dream a reality.

It's easy to get distracted by the smallest things such as emotions, social media, or even a loved one, but it will be up to you to direct that focus back to where it was before.

Distractions are placed on Earth by the enemy to detour you from your goals. The enemy wants to see how long he can distract you. The more you focus on the distraction, the longer it will take you to reach your place of destiny. It is very important not to lose sight of where you are going. If you focus on the distraction too long, you may end up in a place that you never intended to be.

Place your focus on God and not the surrounding commotions of the world. Whenever it seems you are being distracted remind yourself, "Lord this is for your glory, and through it all I will remain focused." There's that pep talk again. Just like you reminded yourself on Day 4 to stay encouraged during feelings of defeat, you can remind yourself to not lose sight of the goal ahead. You have to get into position, and stay there in order for God to bless you the way you want to be blessed.

Don't worry about tomorrow, instead focus on today. Tomorrow is already handled.

God needs to keep your attention so you can continue moving towards that goal.

You should be so focused that you don't notice when you're being distracted.

Remember the longer the distraction, the longer it will take you to reach your destination. Always remain focused.

What are you focusing on?

What are some of your biggest distractions?

How are you staying focused?

Day 11

Let no one despise you for your youth, but set the believers an example in speech, in conduct, in love, in faith, in purity

1 Timothy 4:12

Leadership

Becoming a leader will not be one of the easiest tasks. Leadership will require you to have confidence within yourself and to be courageous despite all obstacles. You may feel fear, but that does not mean that you have to bow down to it. Leaders take on a great responsibility, such as having others depend on you to answer questions when inwardly you are unsure of the answers yourself.

I remember when I first got my full time position as a Lead Consultant. I was a little afraid because it was my responsibility to direct others. My job required me to manage the floor, the flow of production, and lunch and break schedules. I enjoyed the job, but I didn't like the idea of telling other adults what to do. I was uncomfortable with bossing others around because I didn't want to make anyone feel upset. My job required a lot of responsibility, and an abundance of confidence from me. One day after having a talk with my boss, I realized that if I appeared uncomfortable as a leader then I would make my employees feel uncomfortable as well. I knew that I had to start leading by example, and having a lack of self-confidence is not something that I wanted to display.

In order to be a leader, you have to be strong. You have to listen to that small voice inside of you that is dying to take charge. A leader does not display signs of fear because a leader knows that there is a solution to every problem that is encountered. Although many skills are required to be a successful leader, one of the most important is a strong belief in yourself. When fear says, "No you can't," say, "Yes, I can." When doubt tells you, "Turn away," you tell doubt, "I'll stay." When someone tells you that what you are aiming for is impossible, show them why it is possible.

Leadership is a characteristic of a dreamer, a go-getter, a risk taker, and if you would like to develop those characteristics, you need to lead yourself towards God. You need to get in alignment with obedience. God has so much in store for you if you would just let him lead you.

It doesn't matter how tall you are nor does it matter how old you are because leadership does not have a specific profile description. It certainly does not discriminate. Anyone can become a leader regardless of race, ethnicity, or religion. Every morning you should wake up and think, "I am a leader, and I will lead myself to victory." Don't be a follower; be a leader! Just because you live in the world doesn't mean you have to follow the world. Be wise and make your own decisions, and always remember that a leader will never follow the crowd because he or she is too busy walking ahead of the pack.

Do you consider yourself a leader, or a follower? Why?

What characteristics do you think a leader should possess?

Day 12

How long will you lie there. O sluggard?
When will you arise from your sleep?

Proverbs 6:9

You

Whenever you have an idea in mind, most times the worst distraction is you. How many times have you said to yourself, "I'll do this tomorrow?" Then when tomorrow arrives, you repeat that exact saying again. When you realize that this has become habitual, at some point you're going to have to make tomorrow come today. You can't allow laziness to control your body, and you certainly can't allow it to control your mind. You were given authority over your thoughts and feelings, so that you can control them. They were not created to control you!

Whenever the thoughts of "This can wait, I'll do it tomorrow, or I don't feel like doing it now" come to your mind, make those words submit to you. What if God didn't feel like blessing you today? What if God suddenly didn't feel like he wanted to answer your prayers? Wouldn't you think that was unfair? Well, how do you think he feels when you don't utilize the talents that he gave you? You are talented, intelligent, creative, and wonderful. That's just to name a few characteristics that God has given you. He would like for you to use those characteristics to the best of your ability. Don't let your dreams get away because the laziness in your mind is telling you to put it off for another day.

One of the key words to becoming successful is *consistency.* Consistency is required when you are trying to obtain a goal. You must work towards your goal every day. Once I decided that I was going to follow my dreams of becoming an author, I worked towards that goal consistently. Despite what mood I was in or how tired I was after work, I would come home, and write a few pages each day. I knew that staying consistent would get me to where I wanted to be. I was aware that if I continued writing that I would soon have enough pages to create a book. I could have went out to parties. I could have come home and watched TV every day, but I did not allow myself to lose focus. I did not allow myself to keep myself from pursuing my dreams. I could have submitted to the thoughts of giving up, but there is no room for procrastination, when you are trying to obtain your goals.

Focusing on your past experiences is something else that can hinder you from being who you were designed to be. Some people become so fixated on their past, that they forget they have a future. Some people are so focused on the hurt others placed on them that they carry that hurt into their future, and as a result they become distrusting of others. Forgive those who hurt you, and move forward. You will feel the pleasures of joy when you remove grudges and free yourself of any negativity that is keeping you stagnant. Life is not going to give you any hand outs, so if you wish to accomplish anything you will have to go out there and do it yourself. If you think the world is going to give you something, not only will you be broke financially, but you will be broke mentally as well.

You were created by God so you were amazing as soon as you joined earth. Don't let YOU stop YOURSELF from getting to where you need to be. Pursue whatever desires linger in your heart. When you don't submit to those thoughts of laziness, you will be able to enjoy what you never stopped yourself from doing, and that's living your dreams.

What do you think you are stopping yourself from doing?

What have you accomplished so far?

List 3 great characteristics about yourself

Day 13

For am I now seeking the approval of man, or of God? Or am I trying to please man? If I was still trying to please man, I would not be a servant of Christ.

Galatians 1:10

Opinions

Whenever you are mentioning your dreams in life to others, no matter who it is, be it mom, dad, stranger, or friend, they're going to have an opinion about it. Those opinions can either motivate you or discourage you. People will only give you an idea of how you should strategize your goals from their perspectives. The gist of the idea is that it is from *their* perspective. You have to remember that it is your life that you are living. You are still required to do whatever works best for you. The advice and opinions from others can help you make a decision; however, you shouldn't allow the final answer to be from a choice that was made from someone else other than yourself.

What if Jesus would have listened to people when they were accusing him of not being the son of God? Do you think he would have succumbed to the pressures of others just so they could be satisfied? Jesus believed in himself. He was positive that in order for him to save our souls that he had to die on the cross regardless of what any human being said. He believed in himself because he knew that he was the son of God even when others didn't believe so. You should take a lesson from Jesus, and live life with so much confidence built inside of you that even when the opinions of others try to push you around, you still stand your ground.

There are two types of people who give opinions: 1) those who didn't follow their dreams and 2) those who want you to follow your dreams. Those who didn't follow their dreams may say things such as, "I wouldn't do that if I were you", or they will give you a story of someone who tried it and failed. Don't be discouraged by them. Those people were too afraid to finish their goals, so they will do anything in their power to have someone sit beside them on the, "I didn't make it because I didn't try," bench. Don't sit on that bench! Tell them you have other plans, thank them anyway, and proceed to your destination.

You also have those who want you to follow your dreams. These people will give you genuine feedback after you express your ideas to them. For instance they may say something like, "I always knew you could do it, or you can do anything that you put your mind to."

These individuals are usually close friends or relatives. You need good motivation like this in your corner. The opinions of others should not discourage you. You were born with two ears, so that negativity can go in one ear, and come out of the other one. Opinions will only matter if you allow them too. After all, having an opinion from God is the only opinion you need.

List opinions you have heard from others.

How do those opinions make you feel?

What are you doing to drown out those opinions?

Day 14

Do not withhold good from those whom it is
due, when it is in your power to do it.

Proverbs 3:27

Giving

If everyone on Earth had the heart of mother Teresa, I wonder how much poverty we could prevent. How many children could we save from starvation if everyone joined in to give effortlessly? When you give to people, do it genuinely, openly, and from the heart. You shouldn't give for the sake of receiving praise from others. You should give because it makes you feel great to make a positive impact on someone's life. Some people give with the expectations of receiving something back in return. There are going to be people who are less fortunate than others, and they will not be able to give back, but that doesn't mean they don't want to. You have done your part in giving to them, and honestly that's all that really matters.

There was a period in my life where I completely stopped giving my hard earned money to the less fortunate because I'd made an assumption that they would only buy drugs or alcohol with my money. I had no proof to make such assumptions, but I did it. It wasn't until later in life when this gentleman was in the parking lot of my job begging for money. He had on a tattered shirt, dingy shorts, and overall he did not look to be in good shape. He had the appearance of a man who had been lost in the woods and traveling for days. As I pulled into the parking lot, he came to my window and said, "Ma'am, I just got robbed, and the people took my glasses. Do you have money, so that I can get new eyeglasses?" I was terrified because he was standing at my car, so I had no idea of his intentions. Thoughts ran through my mind like "What does he want? Did he really get robbed? Is he trying to rob me?"

I just looked at him and simply said, "I don't have any cash." That's when he asked for my debit card. I immediately stopped talking and went inside. What sane person would ask for another person's debit card? Meanwhile the guy was still standing outside approaching customers, with his sob story, as they entered and exited the building. When I checked this customer out at my register, I asked the lady if she believed in the sob story that he was telling to everyone. She replied with, "Well, What he does with the money is not for me to know. If my husband knew that I didn't help that man out there, then he would be quite upset. I did my part in giving."

Wow! Talk about a wakeup call for me! From that day forward, I removed all negative thoughts about the less fortunate from my mind. Who was I to judge them? I didn't know their story, so why should I make up one for them? I had the money to give, so why not give it? Why not be a blessing to someone who needs it? I can get my money back from the next pay check, while they are forced to wonder the streets daily in hopes of at least receiving a dollar worth of change to make it through the day. Those are some of the things you should think about when you're giving to others; it doesn't have to always be gifts or money. It can be words of encouragement or a smile to brighten their day.

If you see someone who seems down, pull them into your peace by encouraging them that everything will be just fine. Those simple words can mean a lot to a person who has had a tough day.

Your spirit feels all of the giving that you are doing towards others. This then opens doors for you to receive more blessings for being generous. Think of them as a Thank you Gift from God. You may not be rewarded from people on earth for the good that you do, but you will be rewarded by God for your kindness towards others.

God did not bless anyone on Earth with a selfish spirit because giving is what makes the world go around. How do you think you got here? Your mother gave birth to you. How was she able to do that? God gave birth to her! Giving to others is an essential part of life. Today I challenge you to give. It can be money, words, or gifts. As long as you do it genuinely, openly, and from the heart. Despite their story just know you are doing your part.

What was the last item you gave to someone?

How did that make you feel?

Why do you think it is important to give selflessly?

Day 15

And his affection for you is even greater, as he
remembers the obedience of you all, how you
received him with fear and trembling.

2 Corinthians 7:15

Obedience

Obedience can appear unexciting when you see those around you engaging in "fun" activities that would make a nun squeal. It can make you want to join the fun until your spirit pulls you in the other direction because deep down inside you know that's not the path that you should go down. The world is filled with so many temptations that can easily influence you if you allow them. You have to be confident that you have the strength to do right when wrong is standing right beside you. God is on your side. He wants you to triumph over the negativity, and stand firm in obedience.

When you truly have the fear of God in you, your spirit will automatically follow his commands. That same fear is similar to having the fear of your parents when you were younger.

Growing up, you knew that if you disobeyed your parents sooner or later you would pay for it. They may hold out on your allowance money for the week or keep you away from the television for a certain amount of time as punishment for disobeying them. You knew if you obeyed them that you wouldn't have to deal with the consequences of misbehaving.

Just like your parents rewarded you for your good behavior, God wants to reward you as well. Sometimes you may feel like you are getting blessed without actually being deserving of it. That's just God showing you the love that he has for you. His love will not decrease when you disobey him because he knows that it is not you causing yourself to solely stray away from him, but it's the desires of the flesh that may cause you to do so.

You may think that you have self-control over your mind, body, and soul, but when you are dealing with spiritual warfare, you're going to need more than yourself to win.

Your obedience needs to shout louder than the urging to stray away from the word. Whenever that feeling comes along, remind yourself why you are eager to follow the Lord's footsteps. Listen to the Lord, and let him guide you towards your destiny. God will have so much favor over you when you do things correctly. Your obedience will be rewarded in more ways than you can imagine. God will be so pleased with you. He will rain down so many blessing on you that you may drown in them. Continue to be on your best behavior, and watch God work!

Why do you think it is important to remain obedient to God?

Have you ever strayed away from God's word? When?

What made you direct your path back to obedience?

Day 16

Have I not commanded you? Be strong and
courageous. Do not be dismayed, for the Lord
your God is with you wherever you go.

Joshua 1:9

Change

Change is one of the most uncomfortable life experiences that everyone will go through.

No one wants to be shifted from a place of comfort to an unknown territory that you have to learn to adjust to as time goes by.

Although change makes you feel uncertain about some aspects of life, you have to endure it in order for you to grow. You can't stay stuck in one spot forever. If you do, you'll never be able to utilize your strengths to their fullest potential. Most times you can stagnate your growth by trying to maintain a firm grip on what's familiar.

Let's take a look at 11 year old Caroline; she had a favorite pink shirt that she only wore to big events that she attended. On her 12th birthday, she began to notice changes within her body.

She noticed that the shirt no longer fit her anymore. She tried to squeeze the shirt over her head, but she realized it was too tight! It did not fit because she had outgrown it. This is exactly what happens in life. You outgrow certain people, but you still try to fit them into your life even when you know it's time to let them go.

Change is not always unpleasant. It appears to be in the beginning, but that's just because you don't understand why it is occurring. It's not meant for you to understand the beginning confusion that change brings. You just need to trust and believe in the process with hope that all things will come together for the purpose of your good.

God does not bring change into your life to hurt you. He brings it here to shape you and mold you so that you can learn how to adjust to change no matter how difficult the circumstances may appear to be. Change is inevitable, and it's something you have to learn to accept.

The more you run from it, the more difficult it will be for you to face it. It will be challenging for you to understand that growth is the companion of change. It removes you from a place that you want to be to a place that you need to be.

No one understands what's best for your life the way that God does. Change will increase your perspective on life, and give you new insights on how to handle obstacles as they appear.

Don't run from it; embrace it because in the end the confusion that was felt prior to change will turn out to be the most beautiful process that you could ever go through.

When was the last time you had to adjust to change?

What change do you need to make in your life now?

Day 17

The heart of man plans his way, but the
Lord establishes his steps.

Proverbs 16:19

Future

You will never be able to understand the power of your future if you continue to place yourself in the same situations that can hinder you from it. If you are consistently looking behind you, then you'll never see what's ahead of you. Don't allow yourself to make eye contact with that dark place; walk towards your light. Illuminate your flame by believing that the efforts that you put forth today will be worth it tomorrow.

The future is never as far away as we think it is, but you will need patience and commitment to enter into it. God did not place the characteristic of failure inside of you. He wants you to have the success you have always dreamed of. He wants you to use the fruits of your destiny to help guide you to a place of pure and total bliss.

You have so much in store for you! If you were able to take a peek into your future, then you would do whatever it took to make sure you got there. Not only do you need patience and commitment to get to that place of purpose, but you also need strategy. Without strategy how can you feel motivated enough to strive towards what you want to achieve? If you can envision the end results before you began, then you would be more eager to complete whatever goal is desired within your heart.

Your future lies in your hands. It is important that you make wise decisions and that they are led by God. If you stray away from what God has planned for you, numerous obstacles can occur such as your destiny never being fulfilled, or you could end up living the life that you told yourself you would never live.

You don't want to look back on the last 10 years of your life and think if you would have done things differently then you wouldn't have ended up in a certain predicament.

Don't be the person who grows up and lives a life full of regrets. Push yourself to be consistent and to align your thoughts with your actions. When you get discouraged, remember that you can do all things through Christ who strengthens you and I do mean ALL THINGS!! The future is awaiting you, so don't be the one to let it down.

If you could go back in time, what is something that you would want your past self to tell your future self?

What are you hoping to accomplish in the future?

Are you trusting God with your future?

Day 18

Likewise the spirit helps us in our weaknesses. For we do not know what to pray for as we ought, but the spirit himself intercedes for us with groaning too deep for words.

Romans 8:26

Prayer

Sometimes when you are experiencing mental turmoil, you won't always know exactly what it is that you need to pray about or how to pray about it. The pain may feel so deep and heart wrenching that all you would want to do is cry. Not all prayers are audible prayers, meaning that you don't have to speak in order for God to hear you. Your tears are a sign that you are in need of his presence as well. He knows exactly what it is that you are going through before you mention it to him.

Whatever problems you are dealing with, you should take it in prayer to God. Don't go to people with your issues because they have problems of their own that they can't fix. Don't expect social media rants to make you feel better either because you will have others in your business thus creating an even bigger issue than you had before. Turn your problems over to God, the resolver, and the solution finder because he is the ONLY one who can help you.

Bishop Joseph Walker III from the Mt. Zion Baptist Church in Nashville, TN stated one Sunday that, "People may be too busy to deal with your issues, so they may not be able to respond to your text messages or emails right away, but if you get down on your knees and pray, God will respond quickly to your knee mail."

God may not always answer your prayers as swiftly as you would like, but that will not stop them from getting answered.

When you pray you have to pray consistently without ceasing. Every time the thought of what is bothering you crosses your mind you should pray about it. We go through a period in our lives where we enter "Prayer Season". That is the season where you pray continuously even when there is no indication of any results happening yet. You should praise God as if your prayers have already been answered. Have enough confidence in God to know that whatever you ask for shall be given unto you. Let prayer be a part of your daily life, and remember that you don't need to speak to be heard. Your heart will speak for you.

How often do you pray?

Do you think that is enough time? Why?

What significant thing are you asking God to do for you in prayer?

Day 19

But seek first the kingdom of God and his righteousness,
and all these things will be added to you.

Matthew 6:33

Settling

Many times you can miss out on the life that God has prepared for you when you begin to settle into your own thoughts and plan life according to your wishes.

When you don't seek God for direction of your life, it's almost as if you are implying to him that you do not need him. When in reality you will need him more than you know because not every obstacle that comes your way is a handle it yourself kind of thing. You will need the strength of your Father to get you through any situation that you do not have the strength to get through yourself.

Settling in any aspect of life may lead you to confusion and unhappiness. If you ever have to ask yourself, "Am I settling?" Then more than likely you are. You deserve to have more than a minimum wage job. You deserve more than going an entire year without traveling to one state for the summer.

Most times people settle because it's the easy way out. They don't feel the need to reach for more, so they take whatever is handed to them.

For instance, they know a certain individual wasn't right before they married them, but they stay because to them having someone is better than not having anyone at all. They learn to adjust to the love from that person while knowing that is not who they prayed for. They may become unhappy and ask God, "Why is this happening to me? This is not what I asked for?" They have to understand that God didn't do it, but they did it when they decided to take matters into their own hands and settle.

What is it that you're settling for right now? What is it that you are holding onto? What is it that you are waiting to happen?

God did not intend for you to live a "settling" life. He wants what's best for you and for you to get settled once you are content and have fulfilled the goals that he has prepared for you.

Always seek God for direction and instruction in your life before you begin to make those plans yourself. When you ask for help, sit still long enough to hear his reply back to you. He will not tell you to settle. Instead, he will guide you to a life so prosperous that you'll be glad you followed through with his plans instead of your own. Settling will not be an option when God is involved.

What is it that you're settling for right now?

In what ways can you prevent yourself from settling?

Day 20

Do not be anxious about anything, but in everything
by prayer and supplication with thanksgiving
let your requests be made to God.

Philippians 4:6

Patience

I understand that this is the generation of anxiousness. Everything is so advanced to the point where we don't have to wait for anything anymore. We can text someone if we want a response quickly. We can receive direct deposit if we don't want to wait on a check. This is the generation of Now! Now! Now! Without the anticipation of waiting.

Patience is everything, and it will require total commitment from you. You have to be patient with God while allowing him to answer your prayers. You can't rush him to answer them on your timing because then you could delay any blessing that he had for you. Anxious decisions cause destructive actions meaning your mind isn't sober enough to make clear decisions if it's too drunk from impatience.

If you go on a car lot with impatience in your mind for the need of a new car, you may end up with a beat up car that will have to be taken right back within two weeks of purchasing it. When you go on the car lot with a patient mind set, you are giving yourself time to look around at the different options. The car salesman won't be able to just sell you anything because you're not impatient enough to fall for it.

Nothing in your life should be rushed because the scripture says to not be anxious for anything. Whatever is meant to happen in your life will happen for you. You don't need to rush because it will all unravel itself naturally. It can happen a week or maybe even a month from now, but just know that it is already done.

Besides, why would you want to be impatient? Did you know that impatience comes with side effects such as worrying, stress, poor reactions to choices, and anger?

You don't want to add those issues to your life. Learn to be patient. Make patience a priority. Whenever you feel that impatience rising up in you, command it to simmer down! Relax, don't get all worked up over nothing! Pray often, give thanks, and practice patience. Patience will increase your peace and decrease your worry. All you have to do is try!

What are some things that make you impatient?

How will you practice patience?

Day 21

For I know the plans I have for you, declares the Lord, plans for welfare and not for evil, to give you a future and a hope.

Jeremiah 29:11

Destiny

When God is getting ready to elevate you to your place of purpose, don't be surprised when certain people get cut from the final round of your life. Not everyone is meant to go through the entire journey with you. Some will get dropped off along the way, others will walk away on their own, and some won't begin the walk with you. Be thankful that God is removing the snakes from your garden before you begin to grow.

You don't need anyone around that can cause a delay to your destiny. No man can stop God's plan; however, if you allow the wrong people to have influence over you and your actions then those plans can take a detour. You should develop self-discipline, so you may learn how to control the crowd that is around you.

Not everyone that you have faith in will have faith in you. Not everyone that you are honest with will be honest with you. When certain people begin to disappear from your life, don't be alarmed. That's just God's way of doing a little spring cleaning.

God knows the plans that he has for you, and he certainly knows what you are capable of doing. He has chosen you, and only you to complete your earthly assignment so that you can return to his kingdom of heaven and dwell in righteousness.

Although you are born with destiny, you can also miss out on it if you decide to chase anything else but God. People play a major role in your destiny because they can become a distraction if you allow them too.

Don't be afraid to let God use you, even if it means that you have to cut communication with certain people in your life, and step out of your comfort zone. Your destiny requires certain types of people to be involved in your life so that they can motivate you along the way.

Pray for those who enter your life, and ask God for wisdom on whom to remove. Your destiny is out there waiting for you, so what are you waiting for? Go get it.

Who are you taking with you on your Destiny Bus?

Is there anyone you need to remove from that bus?

What do you think can hinder you from reaching your destiny?

Day 22

For to set the mind on the flesh is death, but to
set the mind on the spirit is life and peace.

Romans 8:6

Peace

Outside of your gate of peace are people, circumstances, and situations standing and just waiting for their moment to attack. It always seems that when you are content, and focused that those outside forces try to find a way to destroy your peace. Don't allow them to! Don't give those things the satisfaction of destroying your internal happiness.

When you feel like you are being attacked, remember to call on God. He is your soldier, your refuge, your lawyer, and your defender. He is only one prayer away and available to you 24 hours a day.

God wants you to be in peace. He wants you to be content with life and worry free. He understands that each new day comes with new sets of problems, but you don't have to worry because he has already saved the day for you.

Your peace is yours. No one can take that away from you unless you give them the power to do so. You should be aware of the people in your life who are "peace keepers". Those are individuals who try to keep your peace without giving any to you. If you know someone who can ruin your day when they call you then don't answer the phone. If you know that one individual at your job who finds a way to ruin your day then don't allow them. Just speak, clock in, and get to work.

You are not obligated to entertain anything that will cease your peace. Your time on Earth is valuable. You don't know how much of it that you have here, so it's best to take in all the happiness that you can while you can.

You can't control how others will treat you, but you can control how you respond to them. If you remain upset and frustrated, it can cost you your entire day; however, be mindful that peace is free. You can keep it for the rest of your life.

God wants you to remain in peace not in pieces. He is available to you 24 hours a day all you need to do is pray.

List things/people who disturb your peace.

How can you stop them from keeping your peace?

Day 23

For the Holy Spirit will teach you in that
very hour what you ought to say.

Luke 12:12

Inspire

Throughout the bible, you may have noticed how God will use people to inspire others. He used Jonah, and most importantly, He used Jesus as evidence of his existence. He has also used David to show proof of courage, King Solomon to show an example of wisdom, and Abraham to show the validation of faith.

These people may have been utilized in different ways and in different time periods, but what they have in common is that they were all used by God for their own unique purposes.

You too can be utilized by God to inspire others. You don't have to be afraid of steering someone the wrong way. You don't have to be fearful of not knowing what to say. God will equip you with courage, wisdom, and faith to do whatever it is that he needs you to do.

Inspiration is very captivating because you could be inspiring someone without actually being aware of it. You will never know who you are motivating. You may be someone's muse, even when you feel like you are not giving life your best shot. You aren't always aware of who is watching you.

If you knew how many lives were inspired by your accomplishments, and strengths would that give you enough motivation to push through life when hardships come about? Did you answer yes?

If so, you should know that God is already watching you. He is your biggest fan, and if that isn't enough indication to get your motivational juices flowing then I don't know what is.

Let God use you as an example to inspire others. Take the time today to go out there and inspire someone or even yourself.

You will never know how much motivation is needed until you begin to give it. Leave a lasting impression on others by becoming an all-around inspiration in every area of life. You have to leave your footprints behind, so when your visit from Earth is over, people will always be in remembrance of how you made them feel. Be inspiring!!

Who or what makes you feel inspired?

Who in your life are you inspiring now?

Day 24

9 Let love be genuine. Abhor what is evil; hold fast
to what is good. 10 Love one another with brotherly
affection. Outdo one another in showing honor.

Romans 12:9-10

Family

Your family is the glue that will hold you together when you feel as though everything is falling apart. They are your support system when you need the encouragement that you can't seem to give yourself sometimes. Your family is the true definition of love.

Sometimes we get so swamped in our everyday lives that we forget to show love to those who love us daily. We forget to call and check on grandma or our parents. We forget to acknowledge the importance of their presence in our lives. Although they may not hear from us every day, our parents and grandparents know that they are loved.

On the days that God does not hear from us, He knows no love has been lost for him. You have to make time in between your days to talk to him. You have to create time in your days to pray to him. There shouldn't be an excuse as to why you can't acknowledge him with love daily.

Your family will believe in you when strangers don't. Your family will love you even when they have seen you at your worse behavior. They will always stand by you when you're doing right. They will also be there for you to let you know when you are doing wrong.

Time is too precious and valuable to not spend it with the ones you love. Whatever grudge you may be holding against a family member of yours, just let it go. Grudges are the enemy of peace. They cannot stand in the same room together because one will always try to overpower the other. God wants you to forgive and love everyone, so if you are still holding a grudge A.) You have not forgiven them. B.) If you have not forgiven them, then you certainly aren't showing any love.

Today, take the opportunity to call your loved ones. Check on them to see how they are doing. Ask them about their day. Take the time to discuss whatever issue is bothering you, so that issue can be resolved immediately. Your family is love, and you need them because I don't know what birdhouse can be held together without its special glue.

Which family member did you call today?

Did you resolve any issues?

How does that make you feel?

Day 25

And after you have suffered a little while, the God of all grace, who has called you to his eternal glory in Christ, will himself restore, confirm, strengthen, and establish you.

1 Peter 5:10

Suffering

Why me Lord? What did I do so wrong in my life to deserve this? Those may be the questions that go on in your head in the mist of your suffering. God is not punishing you because you did something wrong, No, he does not operate that way. His intention for your suffering is not to harm you, but to help you. He wants to help you to grow in strength. He wants you to learn how to trust him when you can't find the reasons why you should. He also wants to know if he can trust you while you are going through it. He wants to know that you will trust him when things are going bad, and not just when they are going good. God wants this to be a learning experience for you because he knows that you will come out stronger than you were before.

Going through suffering is similar to taking clothes to a cleaners. Let's just say you own a white pants suit or dress that happens to be your favorite. It has ketchup and mustard stains all over it. You hand your suit or dress over to the person at the front counter in hopes that they can clean it for you. In fact, you have faith that they will because they have equipment there that you don't have to clean it with yourself, so you have to get the help from someone else. You know once the item is back in your possession, it will be spotless. It will look better than before.

You're not strong enough to go through the suffering by yourself, so you call on a higher power to assist you. You understand God has equipment that you don't have to aid yourself. God is the only one who can remove the stains and pains from your life. He is the only one who can make you look and feel brand new.

Just like the suit, you will come out so clean that people won't notice what you have been through. Suffering was what you were doing, but it's not who you are. Once you come out of your suffering, you will be able to enjoy life again. You will understand that it was just a minor setback for a major come back. Suffering is only temporary. It will appear permanent when you allow your problems to consume the solutions. Don't allow it to control your mind.

Trust God. When suffering passes over you, you will be wiser than before. You will be made whole again, and just like that suit you will be spot free and clean.

When is the last time you went through a suffering?

How did you overcome that suffering?

Day 26

How long must I take counsel in my soul, and have sorrow in my heart all day? How long shall my enemy be exalted over me?

Psalm 13:2-3

Frustration

When you know God knows exactly what it is that you are going through, it may appear frustrating to count on faith to get you through a situation. It is the thought that he can solve all of your problems in the blink of an eye if he wanted to. He could cease all wars. He could cease all economic crises. He could also cease all the crime in the world if he wanted to. So why hasn't He? When you begin to allow yourself to believe that God's timing is equivalent to man's timing the more frustrated you will become. God's timing is nothing compared to man's. He never does anything without a strategic plan because he knows that in order for one thing to happen something else must take place before it.

Frustrations will cause a delay in your blessings and a halt in your faith. You can't allow yourself to be angry with God. How can you allow yourself to be angry with the Creator of Peace? Frustration is the result of an impatient mind set; although, you may not understand why that devastating change occurred in your life just know that help is on the way.

Remember one thing must take place before anything else can happen. Before there is peace, there must be war. If there is no war, then how can you know about peace? Before there is joy, there must be pain. How can you experience joy without first experiencing pain? Before there is understanding, there must first be frustration. Without frustration, how can you understand what you were frustrated about?

You must not allow yourself to feel frustration for too long. Frustration is a horrible place to stay. If you allow yourself to become a permanent resident, then everything around you will appear frustrating as well. You must give yourself the opportunity to breathe in peace and faith. Don't get consumed in frustrations with life, God, or anything for that matter. Everything will work out in the exact order that it is supposed to. Rely on God's timing and not the timing of man. He knows exactly what He wants to do, and when He wants to do it. You have to refrain from allowing your frustrations to keep you from losing sight of your faith. Life is filled with so many pleasantries when you get rid of frustrations, so smile, and let your faith do its job.

What are some things that make you frustrated?

How do you overcome that frustration?

Day 27

4 Love is patient and kind; love does not envy or boast; it is not arrogant 5 or rude. It does not insist on its own way; it is not irritable or resentful; 6 It does not rejoice at wrongdoing, but rejoices with truth. 7 Love bears all things, hopes all things, and endures all things.

1 Corinthians 13:4-7

Love

....

…..And the greatest gift of all is love! What greater gift could God have given us other than His love? Many people are still searching the Earth lost in hopes of finding it. They are inquisitive about its meaning. If they open the bible, they will find the definition of love right there. Love is beautiful. It is filled with joy, peace, and truth. Love will never fail you. People often get hurt by those whom they love, and as a result of that, they begin to associate love with hurt and pain.

Love does not hurt people. It is people who hurt people. Those who love you will not cause you such agony. Those who hurt you are hurt within themselves. They are dealing with an internal conflict that can only be resolved by making amends to the pain that they are keeping inside. They are dealing with issues that can only be healed with love.

Pray for those people. You must reach out to them in a way that will make them understand that they are not alone. That's what love does. It heals, and it helps. Whatever you do, you must never give up on love. Giving up on love is just like giving up on God because God is love! Be the love that you wish to encounter. Give love freely, and openly to your friends, family, coworkers, husbands, wives, and anyone else who is surrounded in your circle of love.

Once you begin to relax and let yourself give love abundantly, you will see that there is so much joy in that four letter emotion. The more you allow yourself to drown in it, the more of it your spirit will be willing to give. Love will work itself from the inside out if you allow it. Let someone know that you love them today. Let love use you. After all, it is the greatest gift given to man by God, so start sharing the love with those you love and with anyone else who needs it.

What other gift besides love do you think is God's greatest?

Who are some people that you love?

How much love do you have for yourself?

Day 28

Greater love has no one than this that someone
lay down his life for his friends.

John 15:13

Friends

Friendship just like family is another important relationship within your life. You have those friends who have been around so long that they are practically family now. You also have friends that you love dearly just like brothers and sisters because blood wouldn't make you any more closely. True friends are there to help you get through any bad situation in your life. They are also there to help you celebrate when your life is going great.

There will be two types of friendships that you will encounter throughout your life: Seasonal Friendships and Lifetime Friendships. Your seasonal friend will be there just for a moment. They will enter your life, fulfill their purpose, and leave. They are only there briefly to assist you in whatever period of time in your life they were assigned to you. It's not meant for them to stay a lifetime.

Lifetime friends are forever. They will never change on you, and they will always remain loyal to you whether you are right or wrong. They will not gossip about you to others because they respect you enough not to betray you. They know if you all are having any issues that they can come and discuss it with you, and not those who are around you. People make mistakes when they try to turn a lifetime friend into a seasonal one. You can't make that happen because when you hang around someone continuously their true colors will show and eventually their motives.

If you find yourself giving more to a friendship, and it's causing you stress, then let it go. No friendship should stress you out. Be careful of those who only initiate contact when it is beneficial to them. Those people aren't looking for friends; they are looking for help. A friendship should be 50/50. You have my back, and I have yours, not you have my back and I have my back too!

You may not talk to your friends every day, but you don't have to because a lifetime friend will not ask you to keep in contact just to validate the friendship. Good friends will not wait until you've accomplished your dreams to support you. They'll always be there throughout the journey. Thank God for the friends in your life today because without them there is no telling where you would be.

Who are some friends that you can count on?

Why do you believe God placed these people in your life?

Have you ever encountered a seasonal friend?
What did you do about them?

Day 29

If any of lacks wisdom, let him ask God, who gives generously to all without reproach, and it will be given to him.

James 1:5

Wisdom

Didn't you know that having and seeking wisdom is one of the ways to please God? He wants you to be drowned in wisdom, so that you may have the knowledge and understanding while facing difficult decisions in your life. The wiser you are the wiser the choices that you make will be. Your life is already planned out, but that doesn't mean that it will go as you planned.

Often times we stray away from our destiny when we begin to listen to others, or we figure that we know what is right for us. You may think you know what's best for you, but if you don't apply wisdom to your thought process then you are making decisions based off of your desires.

Desires can be dangerous and lure you in because they appear to be that shiny diamond you've been eyeing in the jewelry store window; however, when you get up close you notice that it's just plastic on display. You begin to realize that it wasn't worth much at all. Wisdom will enlighten your perspective of truth and save you from making horrible choices that can impact your life later. Have you ever done something that didn't feel right and you hear a voice inside of you that lets you know you are about to go against your judgment because desire told you so? That was your wisdom speaking to you. She wants to keep you safe and out of harm's way.

You should use your wisdom to seek God and to tap into his spiritual insights regarding the seeds of your life. It is wise to listen to Him because your life can crumble when you lack obedience by trying to live life your own way. Whenever you find yourself stuck in a rut, ask God for wisdom. Ask Him for wisdom on how to handle your finances. Ask him for wisdom on your decision making, and ask for wisdom on how to pray. God knows exactly what you need, but a door will not open unless someone knocks. In other words, He is waiting on you to ask. Desire will fulfill the appetite of your flesh, but Wisdom will fulfill the appetite of your spirit. Seek Wisdom. Don't allow your life to crumble doing it your way. God will always follow through with his plans for your life, all you have to do is ask.

What does having wisdom mean to you?

What are ways that you use your wisdom?

Day 30

23 The steps of a man are established by the Lord, when he delights in his way; 24 though he fall, he shall not be cast headlong, for the Lord upholds his hand.

Psalm 37:23-24

Survivor

You are a survivor! You are a survivor! That's right today we celebrate you because you could have been gone BUT GOD! You could have been homeless BUT GOD! You could have let your problems destroy you BUT GOD! There are many instances within your life where you could have been defeated, and the only person who was able to pull you out was not a family member, not a friend, BUT GOD! So go ahead and give yourself a standing ovation for not allowing your obstacles to win you over. God will give his toughest battles to his strongest soldiers. Although some soldiers may get wounded during the battle, they never stop fighting until the victory is won. The secret to winning the battle of life is to look like you have already won it. You have to look like you know that victory is already on the other side waiting for you. You have to look like a survivor even when you don't feel like you are surviving. You can't look defeated half way through the war! That will just make you an easy target for the struggles of life to defeat you.

God is on your side. He wants you to be a winner. He wants you to win against temptation. He wants you to win against depression. He wants you to win against generational curses. He also wants you to win in spirit. Don't ever be afraid to fight. You have come prepared with the two most powerful weapons. Those two weapons are faith and God. How can you not win with both? God will never set you up for failure; He will always set you up for success.

You must make sure that you keep a winner's mindset. Don't be distracted by defeat.

You are a survivor. Like the old saying goes, "What doesn't kill you, will only make you stronger. The more problems you overcome the stronger you will become. You are a survivor! You are a survivor! That's right, today we celebrate you. Put that perfect smile on your face, go out into the world, and show them what winning a victory looks like.

What are some things in your life that you have survived?

How did it make you feel once you survived them?

You Have Accomplished Your Journey!

Congratulations! You have made it to the end of the journey. Now that you have a better understanding of your goals, and how to strategize them, you can honestly say that you have had your S.H.E today. You can take the time out to write in more detail about your accomplishments in the journal on the next page. You have been excellent, and I hope that my goals for you to feel inspired after each reading, motivated to accomplish whatever was on your list of goals, and for you to feel empowered have been met. Serenity, Hope & Encouragement is all you need to survive daily. Always remember that you can do anything that you set your mind out to do. You just have to be willing to do it. Be blessed!

Journal

Journal

Journal

Journal

Journal

Journal

Journal

Journal

Contact Courtney Brooks

Do you have any questions about the book, author, or do you need more inspiration? Do you want to let her know how *S.H.E* has motivated you? If so, please feel free to contact Courtney Brooks by:

Email
Courtneybwrites@gmail.com

Follow her on Instagram
Courtneybwrites

Facebook Like Page
Courtney B

A Message from the Author:

"There is no such thing as a silly dream. It's only silly when you don't pursue it. Don't limit yourself only to what you can see. There are so many opportunities out there for you. Pursue your goals and strive for more! "

Printed in the United States
By Bookmasters